YOUR
DAILY
RESET

YOUR DAILY RESET

366 Practical Exercises to Reduce Anxiety and Manage Stress Using Cognitive Behavioral Therapy

SETH J. GILLIHAN, PhD

Tarcher
an imprint of Penguin Random House
New York

Tarcher

an imprint of Penguin Random House LLC
1745 Broadway, New York, NY 10019
penguinrandomhouse.com

Most Tarcher books are available at special quantity discounts for bulk purchase for
sales promotions, premiums, fundraising, and educational needs. Special books or book
excerpts also can be created to fit specific needs. For details, write: SpecialMarkets@
penguinrandomhouse.com.

Book design by Angie Boutin

Library of Congress Cataloging-in-Publication Data is on file.

LCCN: 2025007359

Paperback ISBN: 9780593855270
Ebook ISBN: 9780593855287

Printed in the United States of America

1st Printing

The authorized representative in the EU for product safety and compliance is Penguin
Random House Ireland, Morrison Chambers, 32 Nassau Street, Dublin D02 YH68, Ireland, https://eu-contact.penguin.ie.

To Ray Pasi,
with gratitude for your friendship and encouragement

Introduction

Welcome to *Your Daily Reset*, a guide to finding equanimity even when times are hard.

You probably know as well as I do that life is a constant series of challenges. Every day you wake up to a world that is filled with threats and uncertainty. You encounter challenges to your health, struggles with your finances, conflict in your relationships, and the ongoing stress of trying to meet all of the demands before you. Even when there's no problem you can point to, you often might have a vague feeling of anxious dread.

The resulting stress and anxiety affect you in many ways. They show up in your body as tension, pain, or a buzzing sense of unrest. They're evident in your mind in the anxious thoughts that keep you on guard against the next potential danger. They affect your actions and can limit your freedom to do certain activities. When stress and anxiety overwhelm you, it can feel dispiriting, as if they're eating away at your very soul and affecting your entire being.

The far-reaching effects of stress and anxiety suggest that you'll need multiple tools to quiet the storms that steal your peace of mind. These tools are found in the principles that have helped countless men and women for thousands of years all over the world.

Be In Your Life

These principles start with **mindful awareness**: making space for your life to be just as it is. A mindful approach allows you to experience the reality of your life, without dwelling on the past or living in the imagined future. You can drop the fight against things as they are and instead work with exactly what life has to offer. The acceptance inherent to mindfulness is the opposite of passive resignation. It's the resolve to live your life fully and to give everything that life is asking of you.

Mindfulness is often equated with meditation, which is one very good way to practice it. But you'll discover many applications of mindfulness in this daily guide, from simple breath exercises and body awareness to mindful walks and opening to life's uncertainty. Together these practices reveal that peace is less about the things that happen to you and more about how you meet them.

Shift Your Thinking

Mindful presence is the foundation for making peace with your mind, which is captured in the **cognitive** tradition. From the ancient Stoics and Eastern mystics to modern-day psychotherapists, human beings have long recognized that your thoughts can make life much harder or much easier for you.

Unhelpful thought patterns distort the truth about you, other people, and the world. They tell you, for example, that you're weak or unlovable, and threaten you with every bad thing you can imagine. If you believe the worst of what your mind tells you, you'll see the world as overwhelming and yourself as inadequate to respond to life's challenges.

But with practice you can start to recognize thoughts *as thoughts*, not as the ultimate measure of reality. You can take a closer look at the thoughts to see if they're true. Do they tell the full story? Do they leave anything out? Are they biased unfairly against you? When you find that your thoughts are misleading, you can develop new ways of thinking that are a better fit with reality.

Plan Your Actions

Finally, mindful awareness and mental shifts help you to shape your **behavior** in ways that reduce stress and anxiety. You can face the things you've been avoiding, so your life opens up again; in the process, your fears will shrink. You can tackle tasks you've been putting off, thereby lowering the stress that comes from seeing things pile up. You can work more efficiently by starting with small, manageable steps that create momentum and lead to big changes. And you can choose to find the rest you need.

How to Use This Book

In the pages ahead you'll find a short, simple exercise for every day of the year. These practices build on one another the more you use them, so it's best to aim for consistency. The exercises are designed to fit into busy days. Watch out for thoughts like, "I don't have time to pick up that book today." Feeling like you're too busy to take the time is often a sign that the day's practice might be especially needed and helpful. You can always do an abbreviated version that fits your schedule.

If you do wind up skipping one or more days, it's usually best to pick up with the current day's practice rather than going back and doubling up. Less tends to be more as you're applying these skills. On a related note, you can always modify an exercise to make it easier if the full version seems daunting. A little can go a long way.

There probably will be some practices that you especially enjoy and want to return to. You can dog-ear those pages and circle the dates, or use the chart on the following pages to circle the dates that correspond to those entries.

At the beginning of each month, you'll find a longer entry that focuses on a specific concept in mindful cognitive behavioral therapy. These pages are meant to give you additional background and food for thought as you work through the daily exercises. They're applicable any time of year, so feel free to read them whenever you want.

Finally, you can start on any day of the year. The entries begin on January 1, but you don't have to wait for a New Year to get started. When you're ready to begin, the best time to start is today.

I'm really pleased that you're using this book, and I wish you all the best as you get started. May you find growth and new life in the pages ahead.

Favorite Practices

Some of the practices from the year will feel especially resonant for you. Take a picture of those exercises, set

JAN	1	2	3	4	5	6	7	8	9	10	11	12	13	14	15
FEB	1	2	3	4	5	6	7	8	9	10	11	12	13	14	15
MAR	1	2	3	4	5	6	7	8	9	10	11	12	13	14	15
APR	1	2	3	4	5	6	7	8	9	10	11	12	13	14	15
MAY	1	2	3	4	5	6	7	8	9	10	11	12	13	14	15
JUN	1	2	3	4	5	6	7	8	9	10	11	12	13	14	15
JUL	1	2	3	4	5	6	7	8	9	10	11	12	13	14	15
AUG	1	2	3	4	5	6	7	8	9	10	11	12	13	14	15
SEP	1	2	3	4	5	6	7	8	9	10	11	12	13	14	15
OCT	1	2	3	4	5	6	7	8	9	10	11	12	13	14	15
NOV	1	2	3	4	5	6	7	8	9	10	11	12	13	14	15
DEC	1	2	3	4	5	6	7	8	9	10	11	12	13	14	15

them as your phone wallpaper, dog-ear the page, and/or circle the dates on the table below to make it easy to return to your favorites.

JAN	16	17	18	19	20	21	22	23	24	25	26	27	28	29	30	31
FEB	16	17	18	19	20	21	22	23	24	25	26	27	28	29		
MAR	16	17	18	19	20	21	22	23	24	25	26	27	28	29	30	31
APR	16	17	18	19	20	21	22	23	24	25	26	27	28	29	30	
MAY	16	17	18	19	20	21	22	23	24	25	26	27	28	29	30	31
JUN	16	17	18	19	20	21	22	23	24	25	26	27	28	29	30	
JUL	16	17	18	19	20	21	22	23	24	25	26	27	28	29	30	31
AUG	16	17	18	19	20	21	22	23	24	25	26	27	28	29	30	31
SEP	16	17	18	19	20	21	22	23	24	25	26	27	28	29	30	
OCT	16	17	18	19	20	21	22	23	24	25	26	27	28	29	30	31
NOV	16	17	18	19	20	21	22	23	24	25	26	27	28	29	30	
DEC	16	17	18	19	20	21	22	23	24	25	26	27	28	29	30	31

JANUARY

Anxiety Is Not a Personal Failure

Everyone feels anxious at times—it's part of being human. At the same time, anxiety is a private experience that can feel very personal. You might even judge yourself for feeling anxious.

It's easy to see anxiety as a personal failure when there are so many tools available for addressing it (including this book). Maybe you've been to therapy or done a lot of self-help, and you think you should be over it by now. Or you've read the Stoics and practiced meditation, but anxiety still has a firm foothold in your life.

You might even think you're hopeless and that there's no sense in trying to find relief.

But the truth is, no practice or principle will get rid of anxiety for good. Some days you'll feel anxious for no apparent reason. At times you'll worry about things even though you know they're beyond your control.

These bouts of anxiety are not a sign that you're bad at mental health. They just mean you're still alive, and living people are prone to spells of anxiety.

That's why there are 366 entries in this book and not one or twelve or fifty-two, because anxiety tends to be a *daily* experience. Effective practices will help you manage it, but they can't erase something that's a fundamental part of functioning human beings.

So take heart, my friend. Your difficult emotions are not a personal shortcoming. There is no time at which you'll finally solve anxiety or master your relationship with your thoughts and feelings. Let yourself receive the full range of your experience, including the anxious thoughts and sensations that visit you. Make space for all of who you are and what you feel.

Monday – 11/3/25 ✓

A New Year begins. Start where you are.
Feel the breath in your lungs. Recognize any
emotions that are present. Sense where you are,
and who you are. Wherever you go, come
back to this inner connection.

Breathe in for a count of two. Exhale slowly to a count
of four. Repeat, this time in for three, out for six. Do
one more round, four in, eight out. Notice how you
feel. Repeat whenever you need to release tension.

Who do you know yourself to be, factually?

In contrast, what are some things about yourself that
are guesses or accusations your mind makes?

Practice being aware of the difference.

Say no to one thing that would add unnecessary
stress to your day. Replace it with something
you'll really enjoy.

Spend some conscious time outside. See the sky.
Feel the ground. Sense your body as it moves.
Experience yourself as a part of all you're witnessing.

When you get in bed tonight, take ten slow, easy breaths. Let go of something from your day with each exhale. (Place a note about this practice at your bedside to help you remember.)

Bring to mind one thing you're worried about.
Write it in the space below.

Now list everything you can control about it
in the inner circle below, and everything out
of your control in the outer circle. Direct your
energy toward what's inside, and release
everything that's out of your control.

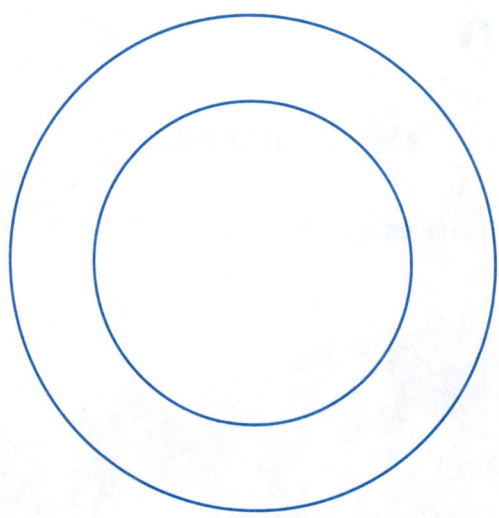

JANUARY 8

When you're flooded with anxiety about the future,
notice the thoughts that fill your mind. Let go of
efforts to force the future to turn out the way you
want it to be. Redirect your energy toward training
the mind in new ways of thinking.

JANUARY 9

When emotions show up throughout the day, allow
yourself to feel them in your body. Remember that
you don't have to get rid of uncomfortable feelings.

Offer more kindness to someone than they seem to deserve. Enjoy giving the gift that everybody wants.

Think of one fear you have needed to face,
such as taking a trip to a new destination.

What do you value more than your fear—
for example, freedom? Family? Courage?

Allow what you love to help you meet
your fear head-on.

On a slow in-breath, feel the front of your
body gently expand. On the exhale, feel it softly
contract. Follow these in-and-out cycles for
several more rounds of breath.

Notice when hopes and wishes are cranking up
your stress, as if you can be OK only if things turn
out the way you want. Can you pause from needing
anything to be different than it is?

JANUARY 14

When anxiety flares up, ask yourself: *What is actually happening right now?* Notice how much simpler it is than all that the mind can imagine.

JANUARY 15

When you feel stress and tension, inhale, make fists, and tighten the muscles in your arms. As you exhale, gently open your hands and relax your arms. Let the stress dissolve as you repeat twice more. End with three slow breaths.

JANUARY **16**

Feel when your mind has drawn your attention to the margins of life, where your worries, fears, and imagined catastrophes are found. Draw it back to your center. Find rest by abiding in this very moment.

JANUARY **17**

Feel the bare reality of what your senses are bringing you right at this moment. Notice how unreal the mind's hopes and fears are. Rest in reality.

18

Come back again and again to your body, feeling
exactly where it is. You can be with yourself, even as
you're moving and taking care of things.

19

Notice the urge to rush ahead to what's next.
Question the thoughts that tell you you're not
going fast enough. You have time.

Describe an upcoming situation that
you've been worried about.

Trying to resolve an uncertain future only ramps up
anxiety, because you don't have that kind of power.
Let go of responsibility that was never yours.

21

Anxiety and stress can lead to chronic seriousness,
which makes everything feel more dire.
Allow yourself to smile. Perhaps it doesn't
have to be so heavy.

22

Close your eyes. Breathe in. Breathe out. Look for
the part of you that is steadfast, even when the
surface of your life feels topsy-turvy.
Drop into your stable core.

Challenge any thoughts that tell you you're not doing enough. How strong is the evidence that you have to be more productive? Maybe you don't always have to do more.

Anxiety may tell you that you need to worry—that worrying will make you safer. See through this lie. Question the premise that it's your job to worry.

JANUARY 25

Take a 15-minute walk outside today at lunchtime, or at any point this afternoon. Notice what the walk and the time outdoors do to you.

JANUARY 26

Turn toward the sensations in your body when you feel anxious. Study the individual experiences that tend to blur together and are labeled as "anxiety"—for example, a tightness in your chest or a lump in your throat. Discover what it's actually like—and that perhaps it is nothing to fear.

Instead of hoping for an easy day, seek the strength
to face whatever comes your way.

Should can be a tyrant. Try trading "I should"
for "I can" or "I will." For example, "I should exercise
more" might become "I will exercise today."
Rewrite your self-talk to reclaim your own power.
You can practice now:

Transform "I should_____"

to "I can/will _____,"

Tomorrow grabs a lot of energy and attention. But an unbridgeable gap separates this day from the next. You can't solve tomorrow, and tomorrow can never touch you. Practice seeing the distance between you and tomorrow, and leave it alone until it becomes today.

Bring your awareness to your hands. Sense the power in them, the energy, the ability to act on the world in meaningful ways. What will you direct your hands toward today?

Anxiety is great at grabbing attention, but generally offers very little useful information. Choose where you direct your mind and energy. What is worthy of your attention today?

FEBRUARY

Letting Go of Unhelpful Stories

Your mind loves stories—so much so that it's constantly inventing stories about what's happening. Some of them are about yourself:

I should be over this by now.
I'll never get married.

Other stories are meant to explain people's behavior:

She cut in front of me because she's selfish and narcissistic.
He's tired of being with me.

Stories about the past trigger feelings such as guilt and resentment:

I wasted my parents' money.
They've never really been there for me.

Future-focused stories can lead to stress and anxiety:

Today is going to suck.
Things in our country will only get worse.

Most of the time we think these stories are real, as if the mind's guesses and interpretations are simple facts about what's true. We believe we actually know that today will be terrible, or that the only explanation for our partner's silence is that they're bored of the relationship.

But reality is much simpler than the stories the mind constructs about them. Maybe the line cutter was confused and not selfish. Maybe your partner is exhausted but is happy to be with you.

A straightforward question can guide you to the simplicity of reality:

What is actually happening right now?

The mental overlay dissolves. What remains is less complicated—the facts of the here and now. And yet more is here than you realized. You can witness all the elements that make up this specific moment, from the air on your skin and the gray of the sky, to the sound of your footsteps and the smell of the winter air.

Ask yourself this question as often as you find that your mind is troubling you with stories. Watch your relationships improve when you see through the fictions that come between you and others. Uncover the false beliefs about yourself—you're not failing, or hopeless, or unlovable.

Start in this very moment. *What is actually happening right now?*

Meet the world today with your chin up and your
head high. Find a sense of nobility in your bearing.
The life you have is yours to live.

Plan to go easy on yourself today. Cut yourself slack
when you make a mistake. Offer compassion when
you struggle. Let your limitations be no big deal.
Smile at every imperfection.

Feel the cycles of breath like waves on the shore. On the in-breath, a wave rolls in; on the out-breath, it rolls back out. Let yourself be moved by the breath. Continue riding the waves for 1–2 minutes.

Acceptance does not mean indifference.
A person can accept bitter disappointment or
a devastating betrayal. Acceptance opens a wider
willingness to experience all of it—the full suite
of the human drama. What are you willing to
feel right in this moment?

When worry asks you, "What if . . . ?," tell it how you actually would respond. For example, "What if it rains?" → "Then I'll need to reschedule." Most worries don't come true, and the ones that do become problems you'll solve.

Catch your mind when it's *shoulding* at others or the world: "You should agree with me"; "This app should load faster." A *should* usually expresses a preference, not a rule that must be followed. See how it feels to swap the *should* for "I wish . . ." or "I would like it if . . ."

7

Notice how often the mind practices fortune-telling today, as if it could see the future. Consider how much of your anxiety comes from those cloudy visions in the "crystal ball."

8

Use each meal as a mindful check-in. When you sit down, take three full, easy breaths. Make the exhales extra slow. Invite peace to join you at the table.

Block out time today to complete one activity that would feel good to cross off your to-do list. It can be as big or as small as you like.

When you're rushing and pressed for time, return to yourself. Breathe in and silently say to yourself, "I am." Breathe out and say, "Here." Repeat this simple statement several times as you establish your place in the present.

Make a plan to spend part of your day with someone who brings out the best in you.

Write down any thoughts you have that
cause you to feel more stressed.

Do they tell the whole story, or do they leave
something out? Are they based on assumptions
that might not be true?

See if there are different thoughts that
might be more helpful and accurate.

13

Notice when you're making an assumption about what someone is thinking—for example, "They think I'm a disappointment." Ask yourself if you know it's true. Remind yourself that you're not a mind reader, and these may be creations of your own mind.

14

Lie on your back. Gently place your fingers over your closed eyes and your palms on your cheeks. Feel the soft pressure on your face and eyelids. Stay here for at least a minute. Receive this touch as an act of care.

Look for a theme that underlies your anxious thoughts. For example, "Nothing good lasts" or "I can't handle it." These deeply held assumptions are core beliefs that give rise to your thinking patterns.

Ask yourself if your core belief is really true. If not, what is another perspective that's a better fit with reality?

When a problem comes up, ask yourself if it's really as bad as your mind tells you. Is it truly awful—a real catastrophe? Or is it a problem you'll deal with like you've handled so many others?

Be on the lookout for black-or-white thinking where you see things as all or nothing. For example, if things aren't perfect, they're *terrible*. Look for all the gray that lies between the extremes.

Place both hands over your heart. Feel the subtle rise and fall of your sternum with each breath. Set an intention to stick close to yourself today.

What subtle rules constrain your actions in ways that aren't always helpful? Look in different areas of your life such as work, relationships, and leisure time. Find out which self-imposed rules need to be broken, and write them out here.

When you're worrying, allow yourself to open to the uncertainty—even if only a little bit. You don't have to figure out the unknowable in advance.

Close your eyes and let the air flow easily in and out of your lungs. Feel the strength in every breath.

FEBRUARY **22**

Treat a problem that arises as an opportunity
to grow, rather than a chance to pass or fail.
What skills will help you to solve it? What might
you learn from it?

FEBRUARY **23**

Give yourself a break from screens sometime today,
even for 10 or 15 minutes. Notice if the peace you
seek is not actually found on a device.

Notice a consistent pain point in your day—for example, having trouble reaching things on a high shelf. How could you reduce this friction in your life?

Notice what your worry is about. What you fear is probably unlikely to happen, but consider if it did. Imagine yourself finding equanimity no matter what may come.

Look at your calendar for today. Where are you most likely to experience stress? Schedule a few minutes after the event to decompress before moving to your next activity. For example, take slow, calming breaths for a couple minutes, or listen to some of your favorite music.

What are you telling yourself that your happiness depends on? For example, you might believe that other people must approve of you.

Consider the possibility that your ultimate well-being does not depend on factors outside your control. You don't have to outsource your happiness.

28

Recognize when you feel the urge to shut down
and put up defensive walls against something
distressing. Gently ask yourself: *Can I open to this?*

29

*(If it isn't a leap year, feel free to skip this exercise, or
complete it on a day when you're feeling ambitious.)*

Choose an activity you've been putting off because
you're not sure how to get started. Reserve time in
your calendar to figure out how to do it.

MARCH

You're Doing Better Than You Know

I've probably never met you, but I can say with confidence: It's not easy being you. No matter what resources or privilege or successes you've enjoyed, being human is hard.

Painful challenges from childhood may have stuck with you, affecting your emotional life and your relationships. As an adult you've no doubt known loss and disappointment. Stress and anxiety are daily companions. You deal with self-doubt. Difficult emotions can come out of nowhere. Your mind can treat you unkindly, plaguing you with harsh self-criticism.

Perhaps you deal with depression or unresolved trauma. Maybe you haven't told even those who love you dearly that at times you wonder if life is worth the pain. Your amazing and beautiful life can also be so hard.

You're intimately acquainted with your faults and short-comings, and you probably think you should be doing a better job at life.

But I'm certain that you are doing so much better than you know.

I understand if my assumption bounces off you, as if there's no way it could be true. But think about what you've been through. You were thrown into this world as a tiny, helpless infant. The early years weren't easy but you made it through. You completed years of schooling, and transitioned into adulthood.

You know better than anyone that life hasn't been smooth sailing the whole way. All of the years have brought challenges and dark moments. At times it's been hard to like yourself. You've had your heart broken. You've pushed through despair. You've fallen down and gotten back up, again and again.

You have not just survived but found ways to enjoy life. You've made friends, shared love, discovered what brings you joy. And you haven't given up, even when it would have been so easy to.

You've persisted through your imperfections and set-backs. You've shown strength and courage again and again.

Be kind to yourself. Life isn't easy. You're doing a good job.

Release fear. Decide who you will be today.
Feel what it's like to say, "Today I will be . . ."

Breathe in. Breathe out. Notice where your body
feels relaxed, or at least less tense. Breathe with
those areas where you feel a bit of ease.

Notice when you're avoiding something
because of anxiety. Note what it is here:

Approach it with "both/and" thinking:
Instead of saying, "I want to do it *but* I'm anxious,"
try saying, "I'm anxious *and* I will do it."

Step into the role of Observer when
difficult emotions come up. Give them a bit
of space as you just watch what they're doing.
The part of you that takes this perspective is not
itself touched by those feelings. Let them be
just as they are as you witness them.

Feel the sensations in your body. Scan from
your toes up through your legs, arms, torso, all the
way to your head. Invite your mind to connect with
your physical self.

Good nutrition is linked to lower anxiety and better mood. Make one small change for the better in your food choices today. For example, eat a little more fruits or vegetables at lunch. Aim to nourish body, mind, and spirit.

Write down how one of your thoughts has
affected your emotions.

Thought: _____ →

Emotion: _____

Repeat twice more today.

Thought: _____ →

Emotion: _____

Thought: _____ →

Emotion: _____

Start to develop a habit of recognizing the
thought-feeling connection.

What tone of self-talk will you plan to use today?
Circle your top three from the list below, or
add your own:

kind   understanding   patient

encouraging   gentle   motivating

inspiring   accepting   supportive

compassionate   empathic   reassuring

respectful   nonjudgmental   hopeful

others:

When you feel overwhelmed, become curious
about all the physical sensations you notice.
Be a nonjudgmental observer of exactly
what's happening.

When you're feeling difficult emotions, ask yourself:
"What is _____ thinking?," inserting your name
in the blank. Observe yourself objectively to see how
your thoughts might be affecting your feelings.

Choose one task you've been putting off because you're afraid you'll do a bad job:

Identify the first small step you'll need to take. Plan a specific time to complete that first step, being sure to do it *imperfectly*.

Reframe something "I" struggle with as something that many people struggle with.

Your problems are less personal than you imagine. Any limitation you experience is shared with countless others.

Shrug your shoulders up toward your ears as you breathe in. Breathe out, drop your shoulders, and relax completely. Repeat twice more. Feel a bit of tension melt away.

Emphasize your power of choice today.
When something minor doesn't go the way
you wanted, look for a space between the
disappointment and your reaction to it. Maybe
the letdown doesn't have to ruin your day.
See if you can choose how you respond.

Play some music you enjoy. As you listen, feel free
to let your body move with the music if it wants to.
Notice what it's like to let yourself be moved.

Plan one activity that will bring a little more fun into your day. Reserve time in your calendar to do it.

Whenever you're waiting—in line, on hold,
at a stoplight—check in with yourself. How are
you doing in exactly this time and place?

Feel water as if for the first time. Notice all the sensations as you wash your hands, rinse dishes, bathe, or take a drink. Let the experience fill your awareness and usher you right into the moment.

When you're caught in the grip of worry, remember that you can't control the unknowable future. Focus on the subset of things that are actually yours to manage. Let go of all the rest.

In the morning, write down two worries about today.
In the evening, write down how things went.
Notice how your fears compare to reality.

Go for a relaxing walk in a park or other green space. It doesn't have to be anything grand—even a few minutes in a neighborhood with some trees can be beneficial. Open your senses to take in what's around you.

As the day begins, check in with your body. Where are you holding on to tension? Breathe in and sigh it out as you ease into your day.

MARCH 23

Notice how your emotions might be coloring your
mindset—for example, expecting the worst when
you're feeling down, or being optimistic when you're
feeling good. See if you can hold your thoughts
a bit more lightly, knowing they are influenced by
emotional ups and downs.

MARCH 24

Make a plan to move your body in a way you find
enjoyable. It might include a new form of physical
activity that you haven't done before.

Choose one task and allow it to take as long as it takes. Release any sense of time pressure or clock-watching.

26

You don't have to hold everything together all the time, as if you're a passenger keeping the plane in the air. Where might you be able to let go and trust that not everything is up to you?

27

When you run into a problem, notice any emotions it triggers. Make space for all the feelings as you breathe with them.

In the evening before bedtime, write down three good things about your day. Let them fill your mind as you go to sleep.

Plan to drop the habitual judgments of yourself just for today. See yourself more as you really are, without labels of "good" or "bad."

Bring your full awareness to a mundane chore, feeling your body move as you complete it. Experience what it's actually like, as if for the first (or last) time.

When a difficulty triggers stress or anxiety, allow it to reveal something good about your life. For example, a long line at the grocery store underscores that you have the ability to buy food. You're not ignoring the challenge, but rather expanding your viewfinder.

APRIL

Opening to Difficult Feelings

If you haven't felt some uncomfortable emotions today, you probably will before the day's over. It's natural to try to push away sadness, fear, jealousy, frustration, fatigue, and other difficult feelings so the discomfort stops.

But pay attention to what happens when you fight against feelings.

Resisting hard things usually just leads to suffering. You can't make the feelings go away, and the struggle against them causes more tension and distress. You might think you should be able to fix your feelings—to erase anxiety, get rid of anger, eliminate jealousy, or stop feeling sad already. Then, when you can't, it could feel like a personal shortcoming.

What happens when you let go of that struggle?

Perhaps you find that it's OK to feel some discomfort. You can save your energy for things you really care about, rather than using it to wrestle with emotions. They can do their thing while you take care of the rest of your life.

You might even discover that your feeling is pointing to something that's worth knowing. For example, I've realized at times that the anxiety and overwhelm I was feeling were because I was fatigued. Instead of trying to distract myself from the feelings, I could take note of them and allow myself to rest.

Your life is about more than trying to control how you feel. You can let your emotions be as they are. Rather than fighting, ask yourself instead: *Can I open to this?* Shift from resisting to welcoming. Open to what's actually happening.

Allow your experience to be what it is. Make room for what's here. It's OK to reside in the beauty and turmoil of a fully human life.

Set aside time to fix one consistent source of irritation in your day, such as a chaotic closet or an overstuffed drawer.

Get in touch with someone you know who likes you and makes you feel alive.

Look at your schedule for today. What could you add or subtract from it to make your day a little more enjoyable?

4

Imagine approaching the end of your time on earth, and you're looking back at how you lived your life. What are the most important things you will want to have done with your time? Some examples might include being present for the people you love or making good use of your abilities.

Take one small step today that will help you live without regrets.

APRIL **5**

Let your palms rest on your thighs. Spend a few
moments listening to what your mind, body,
and spirit are asking for today.

APRIL **6**

Question the *have-to's* of your inner taskmaster.
Who says you "have to"? Maybe you're allowed
to find a bit of rest.

APRIL **7**

Make or buy a food you really enjoy, ideally
something healthy that will help you
feel alive and energized.

APRIL **8**

Practice a mindset that prepares you to meet
whatever happens today: *I can't avoid challenges.
I can choose how I respond to them.*

APRIL **9**

Sit or lie comfortably and close your eyes. Allow the
sounds around you to enter your awareness. Rest
where you are as each sound arrives.

Watch out for accusations that masquerade as questions—for example, "Why did I do that?!" Provide a straightforward answer that treats you fairly, such as, "Because I was exhausted and rushing."

Notice what your relationship with the clock is like. Does it seem to be the enemy? Look for ways to make friends with the time you have.

APRIL **12**

Notice how you decide when it's OK to rest. Is it
determined by whether you've "done enough"? Or
by whether your body and mind need a break? Write
down your ideas here:

Look for one way today to prioritize
peace of mind over constant productivity.

Remember that anxiety itself is not a problem to solve, but an experience to witness.

Set a timer for 3 minutes. Spend this time rubbing any tight muscles in your neck, hands, feet, face, or jaw. Let go of any pressure to get on to the next thing. Focus on the sensations.

When you believe that someone thinks ill of you, carefully look for the source of that impression. Does it really come from the other person? Consider the possibility that it's a creation of your own mind, and that the other person isn't thinking it at all.

At some point today, anxiety is sure to rear its head.
Plan in advance how you will respond with dignity
and honor, including any tools you will use. Write
down that plan here:

Feel within you the strength to deal with hard things.

17

Schedule 5–10 minutes to clear clutter
from a workspace. Take the time you need
to create your best working conditions.

18

Fear of loss leads to anxiety, but the truth is that
everything will vanish at some point—health,
possessions, titles, dreams, life itself. Enjoy what you
have, and hold it all lightly. Loss is the natural course
of things. Live and let go.

The story of your life is less about what happens
to you and more about how you respond.
How will you handle difficulties today?

Find ease in action, like the relaxed wrist of a skilled violinist. Bring a sense of *being* to your doing. Let your efforts be easy.

Rest can feel like a waste of time because you have "nothing to show for it." But pausing is an essential part of productivity. Offer yourself at least 5 minutes of time today with nothing to show for it.

Each time you step outside today, take in all you see. Feel your connection to the world around you.

APRIL 23

Being steadfast in the face of difficulty doesn't mean
you never get knocked down. It means you keep
picking yourself back up. Resolve today to
keep getting up, no matter what life brings.

APRIL 24

When your mind asks a worried "What if . . . ?,"
drop the urge to get in a mental tussle with the fear.
Offer no resistance as you acknowledge, "Yes, that
could happen." You have what you need to deal
with a worry that comes true.

Notice when difficult feelings lead you to go inward, dwelling in mental fantasies about the future. Square your shoulders, lift your gaze, and direct your attention outward.

APRIL 26

Breathe in and sit up straight. Breathe out and give
your full weight to your seat. Repeat three more
times. Allow yourself to receive support.

APRIL 27

Make one small improvement for your sleep.
Some options include: getting in bed a little earlier;
no screens in the hour before bed; making your
bedroom quieter or darker; no alcohol in the evening;
less caffeine; keeping your phone out of
the bedroom.

Your life so far has surely had its share of struggles. Consider all the challenges you've faced in your life—probably even ones you thought you couldn't handle. What are three occasions when you felt overwhelmed at some point, but you kept going?

1. _____

2. _____

3. _____

Remember today that the same strength you've relied on in the past will help you face whatever may come.

APRIL **29**

Challenge yourself to face one manageable fear.

APRIL **30**

What would it be like to rest completely, even
from trying to make your situation better?
Spend a few moments in quiet stillness.

MAY

Making Space for What Life Really Is

One of your mind's favorite pastimes is to imagine how it wants things to go, as if it's writing the script for the movie of your life. But your mind takes great artistic license as it crafts the story of what should happen. As a result, the script is only loosely based in the reality of how things will turn out.

Nevertheless, it can seem as if the fantasies of what you want or expect to happen are actually *the way life is sup-posed to go*.

Naturally you do all you can to shape life according to these hopes and expectations, as if life should be reading from the script in your mind. And of course things turn out so differently from what you had imagined.

The script called for a smooth and easy day, but the washer broke. Your partner was supposed to say, "Thank you for doing the dishes," but apparently forgot their line. Other people should have been cooperative but instead kept getting in your way.

The "director" in your mind can get upset when reality goes off script. "Why can't things just go the way I imagined?" you might protest.

But we can't judge reality against our expectations. Reality is the ultimate truth and standard.

The truth is that we have no idea, ultimately, what any day will bring—for better and for worse. Life is offering you much more than you expect.

The best parts of your life probably weren't written into your mental script. They were more like improv that surprises even the actors.

Rather than trying to make life into your mental image of it, let it be all that it is: wild, beautiful, unpredictable, and not altogether safe.

Life's a lot easier when you're no longer trying to tame the untamable. Let this day be a continuous series of surprises.

MAY **1**

Honor your well-being today. Refrain from pushing yourself beyond what is good for you in the name of productivity. For example, stop yourself from doing that "one more thing" that puts you over the top. Give yourself what you need when you need it.

MAY **2**

It's time for some mindset training. Remind yourself often today: *I can't manage the future or change the past. My responsibility is in the present.* Train your mind to let go of what it can't control.

What future outcomes are you
banking your well-being on?

See what it's like to drop the belief that you can be
OK only if things go the way you want them to.

Remember that the anxieties and stresses you experience are not unique to you. To be alive is to know pain and difficulties. Look for the common humanity in your struggles.

When the surface of your life is troubled as if by wind and rain, find a deeper peace within. Drop down inside yourself and find a core that isn't touched by the outer storm. Rest in the stillness you find there.

Bring awareness to the explanations your mind offers when you mess up. Reflexive judgments tend to blame mistakes on personal deficits, such as being "lazy" or "selfish." Ask yourself if there is a kinder and truer reason for why you fell short.

Set yourself up for success by clothing your mind in helpful ways of thinking, like getting dressed for the day. What is one helpful perspective to adopt as your day begins, and how will it help to orient you in the right direction? For example, you might remind yourself to question unhelpful stories that cause unnecessary distress.

MAY **8**

Feeling anxious can seem like a sign that you need to work on "personal improvement." But keep in mind that anxiety is not a shortcoming. Let go of any automatic judgments about your feelings.

MAY **9**

Look for the bounty all around you. You have enough: air to fill your lungs, light to see, gravity to hold you in place. Witness the abundance.

Choose to drop resistance to anxiety.
Invite it to hang out with you as long as it likes,
while you go about your business.

Think of a situation you've been worrying about. Fill in the pie chart below with all the factors that influence it. Focus on your piece of the pie.

It's not your job to fix anxiety. Challenge the belief that you must get rid of it.

Question each self-critical thought you notice today.

MAY **14**

Shift your focus from trying to fix how you
feel to taking care of the next thing that
needs your attention.

MAY **15**

When you feel overwhelmed, silently say to
yourself, "Just this." *This* moment is all you
ever need to manage.

Feel your feet on the ground
whenever you start to worry.

You don't have to carry the burden of worry. Trade it
for an awareness of all that's happening around you.

18

Sit comfortably, outdoors if possible. Take full, easy breaths. Sense the oxygen becoming a part of you, right down to your cells. Feel yourself as part of the world all around you.

19

Head into your day as if you have nothing to prove and nothing to lose.

Notice when you're expecting something to go badly.
You can write it here:

Think carefully about how strong that prediction
is. Take note of any evidence that suggests your
forecast might miss the mark:

MAY **21**

Aim to make peace with challenging experiences,
including your own limitations. It's OK to be in the
beautiful mess of a fully human life.

MAY **22**

Extend yourself a bit more compassion
than you ordinarily would.

MAY **23**

When you're in the grip of worry, take a gentle breath in and make tight fists. Breathe out slowly and relax your hands. As you do, release the worry.

MAY **24**

The more you resist anxiety, the harder it is to cope with it. Offer more space for anxious feelings and sensations.

MAY **25**

Question thoughts that say you don't belong.
How do you know for sure that they're true? What
suggests they might not be?

MAY **26**

When you find that you're fighting against difficult
emotions, gently shift from resisting to allowing.

Ask not what this day will do to you.
Ask what you will do today.

28

Are your thoughts amplifying the stress in your life? For example, perfectionistic thoughts might create impossible expectations. Take note of them in the spaces below. For each one, ask yourself if there is a more helpful way of seeing things.

Stressful Thought	More Helpful Alternative
Ex: *I have to do things perfectly.*	*I will do my best.*

When you start to worry, release the story. Sense what's real, such as the air you're breathing and sensations in your body.

When the mind starts to swirl, sit or stand with a relaxed, upright posture. Embody the energy of a mountain. Stay grounded as you observe passing thoughts and feelings.

Being human is no easy thing. Be kind to yourself.

JUNE

Seeing Through Thoughts
That Make Stress Worse

Life comes with inevitable demands, from the work you have to do to the people who sometimes make life harder. At the same time, stress isn't just about what happens to you. It also comes from what you believe about what's happening.

Many of your thoughts turn up the volume on unavoidable stress. For example, if you're slammed with things to do and working as fast as you can, your mind might tell you, "You're taking too long!" Now you're dealing not only with all you have to do but with a critical voice in your head and a sense of inadequacy.

If you're about to give a presentation the thoughts might say, "Nobody's going to like it." That prediction about the future amplifies the stress of the talk itself.

With practice, you can turn down the volume on these stressful thoughts. When you're feeling especially tense and stressed, give yourself a moment. Check in with what's on your mind. Are your thoughts making the stress worse?

Take a closer look at what your mind is telling you. Is it completely true? Do you know for a fact, for example, that people won't like your presentation? Consider what evidence from the past tells you.

Most of the time you'll find that the thoughts are only partly true, or aren't true at all. If that's the case, come up with a more helpful and accurate alternative.

If you thought you were taking too long, for example, you can tell yourself that tasks take as long as they take.

Stress is a daily fact of existence. But that doesn't mean it has to overwhelm you. Train your mind to work with you and not against you as you deal with life's demands.

Pause three times today and notice any excess tension in the body. Take a slow breath in and out as you let the tension dissolve, even a little bit.

As your day begins, ask yourself, "What is my peace of mind worth?" As often as you can, choose to say "Oh, well" instead of "Oh no!" to minor daily hassles.

Carefully tend to your thoughts today. Release
unhelpful stories your mind tells you about yourself,
your situation, or other people.

Write yourself a note that reminds you to come back to the present. Post it where you'll see it throughout the day.

5

Pause and breathe when something challenging happens. Open a gap in which you can intentionally choose how you respond.

6

Recapture the energy that's directed at all the externals you can't control. Center your attention on the internal work you need in the moment.

Watch out for the cognitive distortion duo of fortune-telling and catastrophizing. Consider the possibility that the thing you fear won't happen and, if it does, that it won't be as bad as you expect. (Learn more about these and other cognitive distortions in the Appendix on page 265.)

When worry strikes, remember: You have survived every single challenge you've faced so far.

Raise your awareness of reflexive judgments you make, automatically tagging everything as "good" or "bad," "like" or "don't like." See what it's like to observe and experience without those up-or-down verdicts.

Practice giving less weight to your passing thoughts. Many of them are probably not worth taking seriously.

Be exactly where you are, starting right now.

JUNE **12**

Even if someone thinks poorly of you, that doesn't make it true. Write down a negative judgment someone has made of you.

What do you trust to be the truth about yourself?

Cognitive distortion alert: Beware of
overgeneralizing where you expect one difficult
experience to apply to every similar situation.
Could things turn out better this time around?

Notice when you're making a negative interpretation
of a loved one's behavior. Are you positive that
it means what you assume? Consider other
possible explanations.

JUNE 15

Breathe in gently; as you exhale, allow your jaw to relax. On a second breath cycle, let your tongue soften. With a third breath, let go of tension around your eyes.

Write down what you're upset about the next time
you have a conflict with someone.

Now write what you know for certain in the situation,
and what may be a guess or interpretation.

JUNE 17

Release fear about tomorrow. Every scary
tomorrow becomes a today you can handle.

JUNE 18

Drop any preconceived idea about what will or
"should" happen today. Trade the fantasy of
expectation for the fact of experience.

Create room for play: Plan one specific
way to inject fun into your day.

Each time you wash your hands, really feel the water.
Let it remind you that right in this moment you just
might have everything you need.

When you feel overwhelmed by worries and concerns, ask yourself what someone in your life might need. Is it possible to direct a little of the anxious energy toward being of use to others?

Notice when anxiety is coming from a desire for *more*: more time, money, leisure, health, success, even peace. Rest in the reality of exactly what you have—no more and no less.

JUNE 23

When something good happens, notice if the mind tries to minimize it or say it "doesn't count." You might be discounting the positive.

JUNE 24

Loosen your grip on attachments that tie your happiness to circumstances you can't control. Connect instead with the part of yourself that is untouched by any measure of gain or loss. Discover a peace that is not easily shattered.

Bring to mind a challenge you're facing. What is it asking of you: an adjustment in how you think about it? Taking action? Or letting something go?

When you're feeling tense, notice what happens to your breathing. See if the breath can flow a bit more freely, especially if you're stressed or anxious.

Allow yourself to be unsurprised by the problems
you run into. Every day brings unexpected twists
and turns. Adopt a mindset of "Of course!"
when you encounter them.

Is there a task you've been avoiding out of anxiety?
Block out a specific time to complete it. Put it in
your calendar to help you follow through.

JUNE **29**

Find stillness within. Perhaps the peace you're
after is already here—even closer than the breath.

JUNE **30**

Move toward the unknown today. Approach
uncertainty as if it's a new adventure waiting for you.

JULY

The Future Is Not a Problem to Solve

Bring to mind a worry about tomorrow. Maybe it's a trip you're taking, a family member's medical appointment, an issue at work, conflict with a loved one, or anything else. Notice if you feel any stress or anxiety as you think about that situation and all the uncertainty involved.

So much of tomorrow's power to trigger anxiety comes from the gap between what you can *imagine* and what you can *control*. Uncertainty about an outcome that matters to you is a perfect setup for anxiety. The mind can think of every frightening possibility, and yet there's no way to know what will happen or to resolve things in advance.

You want things to turn out well, and yet you're neither

omniscient nor omnipotent. You can't know what's going to happen, and you're somewhat powerless to control something that directly affects your well-being.

But the future is equally powerless to affect you now since it is nothing more than a thought. Tomorrow is still unformed, and nothing can harm you if it doesn't yet exist. Only the present can present you with problems to solve. Future problems are not yours to fix.

When tomorrow becomes today it will offer you problems to solve. Until then it will have to wait its turn. Let it do its worst today. You are completely beyond the reach of tomorrow.

Managing today is enough. When you're anxious about the future, step back into the present. Ask yourself: *What can tomorrow do to me in this moment? Can it touch me in any way right now?*

Any real challenges you face will belong to the present. When they come, you'll have the strength you need to meet them.

Breathe in and receive. Breathe out and release.
Receive reality. Release resistance.

Pursue your daily goals with all your strength—
without attaching your happiness to them. Guard
your well-being from outcomes beyond your control.

Consider if there is a difficult situation in your life that is calling for acceptance. Write down the truth of it as plainly as possible. For example, "My relationship with my father is strained" or "I'm not doing well at work."

Make space for any feelings that come up as you read what you wrote. The best way forward begins with acknowledging what is.

Declare yourself independent from the tyranny of anxiety, which is unfit to be the ruler of a free person. Pursue what matters to you in a way that is most likely to support your unalienable right to happiness.

Come back again and again to the utter simplicity of right now. The mind can hold anxious complexities, but present reality is simple.

Greet every situation as an opportunity to respond.
When challenging circumstances arise, look within
yourself for what you need to handle them.

Write down one of your current worries.

Remember that the feared outcome would not be the end—every good story is about responding to a crisis. Picture yourself handling the situation you're worried about if it were to come true. What steps would you need to take to deal with it?

Immerse your awareness in the infinite array of colors around you. Take in even the subtler shades that tend to be ignored, like the hue variations underneath your fingernail. Notice that your body brings its own palette of colors to the scene.

Bring awareness to the act of drinking water. Feel the glass as you pick it up. Hear the water as it fills your glass. Notice the sensations as you raise it to your lips. Follow the feelings of the water as it enters your mouth and as you swallow. When you're done, see what it feels like to have just taken a drink.

Gently release any belief that life owes you
something. Nothing was ever guaranteed.
See what it's like to treat each moment as
a surprise party for you.

Write down five calamities that you're not experiencing right now—for example, being a refugee or suffering with the flu.

1.

2.

3.

4.

5.

How much better is life than it could be?

Choose a project you've put off because you're not sure how to complete it. Schedule a time to figure it out. Once you commit to tackling it, you're on your way to a solution.

In a few short hours this day will be over—the only time the world will ever know this particular July 13th. How do you want to have spent it?

14

Plan to "waste" part of your day doing nothing productive. Do something with no aim other than enjoyment.

15

Approach the day as if your hands are open, ready to receive what life has to offer. You're neither grasping what you want nor refusing what you don't want. Let life flow through you.

Lay your palms on a flat surface such as a countertop, desk, or floor. Feel the texture, temperature, and solidity. Repeat whenever you need to direct the mind away from worry and ground your awareness in reality.

17

Recognize any struggle you're having as part of your shared humanity. Countless others have similar feelings and challenges. Rather than separating you from others, these difficulties prove that you belong.

18

Guard your peace of mind from others today. Decide in advance that you and you alone are in charge of your ultimate well-being. Direct your mind and actions accordingly.

The life you're living is borrowed. What will
you make of it for as long as it's yours?

Identify a more realistic way of thinking when biased thoughts trigger anxiety. For example, revise your catastrophic predictions or your assumptions about what others think of you.

What might your life look like if you lived from this different perspective?

Take a 10- to 20-minute walk with no rush or destination. Drop all goals and simply be the one who is walking.

Anxiety often tells you that you *should* worry, as if worrying is the best way to keep yourself safe. Trust that you can let go of worry. It serves anxiety but not your well-being.

JULY 23

Expand your view of the world today. Life tends to shrink down to the size of our daily hassles, obscuring the radiant mystery of it all. Look deep into the mundane and notice what emerges.

JULY 24

Notice when your mind is spinning a story. Is it really true, or does it just *feel* like it is?

As you go about your tasks, focus on what you need to do to complete them, and let go of the ultimate outcome. You can control the energy and skill you bring but not the result.

26

Drop the fight against feelings. Find the courage you need to move forward even with anxiety or fear.

27

Find excuses for more physical movement. Even micro sessions (e.g., walking to another room) count. Feel how your body responds to these opportunities.

When you're expecting the worst,
write down the catastrophe you fear:

What is actually the most likely outcome?

29

Tune your mental radar to detect the habitual self-judgments you make. In what ways are these criticisms unfair and untrue?

30

Remember that nothing lasts forever, neither pleasure nor pain. Everything has a beginning and an end. Flow with change.

Before you enter a challenging situation, set an intention to move through it as the version of yourself that you most want to be—for example, strong, open, or wise.

AUGUST

Making Harder Days Easier with *Just This*

When you're feeling overwhelmed, life can seem like a steep climb up a mountain, and you have no idea how you're going to reach the top.

How will you get through the day's packed schedule, or be the parent that your child needs, or cope with unrelenting grief? How can you stay sober when the urges are so strong? How can you deal with the ongoing health struggles, depression, or chronic pain?

Maybe you're saying to yourself, "I can't do it. I'm not going to make it." But still, you keep putting one foot in front of the other, just as you would climb a tall mountain. You don't know how you'll reach the top, but you know you can take this step. And now this one. And this one.

The mind can imagine all sorts of things that are beyond your capacity for coping. At the same time, you have all that you need to handle the actual problems in front of you. You'll take care of them in the same way that your heart and lungs keep you alive, one beat and one breath at a time.

Whatever difficult path you find yourself on, come back to *this*, whatever "this" is.

When everything on your calendar feels like too much, come back to the narrowest slice of time that is now.

When "one day at a time" is more than you can deal with, just ride out this urge.

When all the grief ahead of you feels unbearable, just weep today's tears.

When you're exhausted from parenting, be with this child in this moment.

When the thought of more pain is more than you can handle, breathe through this wave.

When life feels too big, go small. Narrow your view to only what's before you. When a year or a week or a day is overwhelming, be in the now.

What deserves your attention? Just this. What do you have to solve? Just this. What can you really control? Just this.

As often as you feel overwhelmed, say to yourself, "Just this."

Choose one trait you would like to practice today—
for example, patience, kindness, acceptance,
courage, strength, or resilience. Look for
opportunities to put it in action.

Bring curiosity to any difficult emotion. Observe the
interesting set of reactions that this feeling provokes
in your mind and body. See what's really happening
under labels like "anger" and "anxiety."

3

Plan one special activity that you'll look forward to.

Put it in your calendar at a specific time today.

Breathe in slowly, following the full length of the breath. Pause, then let it out slowly as you pay attention to the entire exhalation. Repeat twice more as you join mind and breath.

How can you take good care of
your mind and body today?

Rewrite the story about "intrusions" into your day,
such as a spill to clean up or an unexpected meeting.
Whatever the day brings, see it as *yours*. Even
when it wasn't what you'd wanted or planned,
this is your life to live.

Step 1: In the morning, write down one part
of today that you're worried about.

Step 2: In the evening, write down what happened
with the thing you were worried about.

Did it turn out better, worse, or
the same as you feared?

If the worry came true, note how you dealt with it.

Stay present for yourself and others.

Before bedtime, take stock of the difficulties you've dealt with today. What is one thing you have learned in the process?

Let the light within you shine. There is a you-shaped space in the universe that only you can fill. Bring the full expression of yourself to what you do.

Come back to your body. You have time to be exactly where you are.

Prepare yourself to encounter challenging people today. In place of outrage, aim for acceptance. Acknowledge that people can be difficult, without trying to force them to do better.

Plan to brush off any unpleasantness that someone directs unfairly at you, such as honking at you for no good reason. No one gets to ruin your day. Grant yourself permission to keep smiling.

Catch yourself mid-catastrophizing. Say to yourself: "My mind is creating a catastrophe that probably won't happen." Seeing it clearly helps you to see through it.

Drop the worry about worst-case scenarios. It won't protect you if something terrible happens, and in the meantime, it will steal your happiness.

Your well-being is not on loan from anyone else. Own it. No one can give it to you or take it away.

Look for love: in the actions of others, in the care that's all around you, in your own unselfish impulses to look out for the people in your life. Love is stronger than fear.

Think of one thing you've wanted to do but have held yourself back from. What if you let yourself take the first step this very day?

Take a short walk in a familiar place and look with new eyes. Notice what you've walked past countless times before but never really *seen*. Take in your world.

Write down three assumptions throughout the day that increase your anxiety. Identifying unhelpful thoughts can often break their spell.

1.

2.

3.

When your mind triggers a worry, silently thank it for trying to keep you safe. "Isn't that thoughtful!" you might say. Then let the mind know you don't need to get bogged down in that way of thinking right now.

How can you be of service today, even with the exact same set of issues you're dealing with?

23

Treat anxious thoughts like noise. They'll do
their thing and you can focus on acting
with courage and dignity.

24

Take a long, full breath in through the nose.
Exhale slowly and say to yourself, "Let it go."
Relax the body and invite the mind to follow.

Look for an opportunity to say no to something that's not in your best interest. Reduce the optional stress in your life.

Notice when you feel most alive. How might you find more of that vitality in your daily life?

When you're anxious, shift your energy away from trying to change how you feel. Ask yourself instead what task you need to take care of.

Think of one daily habit you have wanted to build (e.g., meditating, exercising, flossing, journaling). Reserve time in your calendar to complete the new activity every day for the next fourteen days. Keep track of each time you complete it. In two weeks, we will take stock of how it went.

Silently send these wishes to yourself,
pairing each one with an exhalation:

- *May you be happy.*
- *May you be healthy.*
- *May you find ease.*
- *May you know peace.*

Receive the self-directed, loving kindness.

Take a few breaths that are a bit deeper than usual, without any forcing or strain. Breathe in slowly and feel the lower belly rise, then the ribs expanding outward, followed by the chest lifting. Breathe out slowly.

Be choosy about where you direct your energy. Carefully consider how you want to invest your time and effort.

SEPTEMBER

You Have Everything You Need for Today

Notice the thoughts and feelings that come up when you look at the day ahead. Our minds are good at seeing problems, both real and imagined. Maybe you're thinking of all the things that could go wrong: the sickness that will get worse, the work situation that will be a disaster, the weather that will rain on your event.

And while the challenges you imagine seem too big, your mind also tells you that you're too small to handle them. It tells you stories about how you don't have what it takes, how you can't do it, how you're going to fail.

The combination of big demands and little resources

creates a sense of "Oh no!" as if you can't possibly meet the challenges.

Your mind is correct that each day will bring problems. Most of them won't be as bad as you fear. Others might be even bigger than expected. There will be moments when you're pushed beyond your comfort level.

But is it true that these challenges will be too much for you? Consider all the resources you can rely on:

- Your heart, to open to what's in front of you
- Your mind, for thinking and deciding
- Your body, for putting the mind's plans into action
- The strengths that have brought you this far
- The skills and experience you've gained along the way
- The people who are happy to help you

Your mind is so accustomed to the resources you can turn to that it stops noticing them.

You can't know what your days will bring, and nothing says they'll be easy. But you can know that you'll have what it takes to handle them. When you recognize this truth, your mind can shift from "Oh no!" to OK. *OK, this is what I'm dealing with now. This is a problem to solve.* Notice how a weight is lifted with this realization.

Remind yourself as often as needed: *I have everything I need to face this day.*

Offer yourself validation when you're having a tough time: *Yes*, this is difficult. Acknowledge the pain, and the desire to relieve it. Receive self-compassion.

Close your eyes, take a full, gentle breath in, and exhale slowly as you silently say, "One." Repeat as you say, "Two." Continue until you reach ten. Feel what's happening in your body before you move on.

How might you build yourself up with your inner talk?

Throughout the day, notice what brings you alive and what depletes you, and write it below. Be especially aware of any surprises—for example, maybe you couldn't wait for some downtime but wound up feeling bored, or dreaded a social outing and it turned out to be a highlight of your day.

Enlivening	Depleting

Give yourself the gift of attention. Spend some time listening to what your body and mind are saying to you. What do they want you to know?

What would you do today if you cared less about what other people think of you?

Take a walk outside. Pay special attention to the trees you encounter. Study them closely as if it's your first time seeing such things.

Grant yourself grace,
again and again, just for this day.

Pause from the endless pursuit of self-improvement.
Perhaps you're not a problem to fix.

Make room for the complexity of emotions you
experience. Recognize that different parts of you
may have different feelings about something.

When you get a jolt of emotion today, such as sadness, anxiety, envy, or happiness, greet it with curiosity as an intriguing visitor. Receive the feeling without letting it define who you are.

Two-week check-in: How has the habit-building gone? Take note of how many times you completed the planned activity. If anything got in the way, make a plan here for how you can overcome the obstacles.

Look into the distance at the farthest point
you can see. Let your eyes relax. Breathe.

Do one thing today that your
tomorrow self will thank you for.

When you're feeling emotionally off-balance,
pose this question with your name in the blank:
What does _____ need right now?
You don't have to force an answer. Sometimes it's
enough just to ask the question.

Identify a fear that has held you back from taking a bold step forward—for example: *I'll fail and embarrass myself; I don't have enough experience; people will criticize me.* Ask yourself if it might be worth the risk to follow where your heart is leading you.

Notice when you're resisting pain or chasing pleasure. Flight and pursuit often sacrifice your balance. Take a breath and re-assert your equilibrium.

Minimize the time you spend with people
who leave you feeling drained.

Notice when your thoughts tell you that you would
be perfectly content if only you had X. How many
times have you believed that story only to find that
the things you got didn't satisfy in the way you
expected? Perhaps the well-being you're after isn't
found elsewhere, and in fact is already right here.

Pause for a moment and come to your senses.
Write down three things you see:

Three sounds you hear:

Three physical sensations you feel:

Finally, close your eyes and take
three slow, full breaths.

Release self-criticism about having anxiety or other challenging feelings. Catch the assumptions your mind makes about how they're a sign that you're "doing something wrong" or "need to work harder at your mental health." Maybe they simply mean you're alive.

Look at the palm of your left hand. It represents the past. Turn to your right hand, which represents the future. Bring the two together, which symbolizes the present, and place them in front of your heart. Reside in the now.

Aim to work with who you are rather than struggling to become someone different. Who says you are not all right the way you are?

Give yourself a break from trying to "fix" yourself. Settle into each moment, starting with this one. Focus today on enjoyment over self-improvement.

Release any self-judgment about still struggling with aspects of yourself that you want to change. Living well doesn't mean arriving at an endpoint but rather choosing the direction you will go, again and again.

Open to endings today. Welcome the transience of every experience.

Lie on your back with your feet flat on the floor (or bed). Let your hands rest on the floor at your sides or above your head, palms up. With each breath give more of your weight to the floor.

Catch yourself mind-reading. Write down
what you assumed the other person was thinking
(e.g., harshly judging you).

Then, write down five alternatives that might
be on their mind instead (e.g., "What should
I have for dinner?").

1. _____

2. _____

3. _____

4. _____

5. _____

Identify your three most important goals for the day
that you want to accomplish if you do nothing else.
Choose ones you're confident you can reach, and
make them specific so you'll know when you're done.
Direct your time and energy toward these goals.

Bring kindness to the act of tending to your body
today, like dressing yourself, washing your hands,
or applying lotion. Feel the care inherent in
these actions.

OCTOBER

Grant Yourself the Approval You're Seeking

Think about who you look to for validation. Maybe you seek likes and shares on your social media accounts, or you want friends to compliment you for finishing a marathon. Perhaps you hope that your spouse will notice that you did one of their chores.

Some forms of approval seeking can be almost invisible: complimenting people so they'll want to be around you; shaping what you say to make others think well of you; being excessively "nice" so you'll be liked; always trying to figure out if the people closest to you are upset with you.

We all want to be liked, and it makes sense to maintain good relationships with those around us. But letting others determine whether you're OK won't do you any favors.

If your self-esteem depends on someone else's opinion, you've tied your well-being to their thoughts and feelings about you. When they approve, you get a little boost—but feeling good lasts only as long as their favor. If they disapprove of you, you feel disappointed and deflated.

The truth is that no one benefits when you look to others for your sense of value. Their approval usually says more about them than about you, and is a poor measure of your worth. It's also unfair to make someone responsible for how you feel about yourself. It demands from the other person: *I need you to bolster my self-esteem.*

You deserve a firmer foundation for your sense of self. See what it's like when you stop trying to please other people. Focus instead on how you can show up fully as the person you know yourself to be—the person you were made to be.

Free other people from the burden of trying to provide you with what they can never give you. Reclaim your identity. Live your life the way that only you can.

You are responsible only for what you can actually control. Remind yourself of this fact as often as you notice that you're worrying over the future.

Close your eyes and imagine an empty blue balloon. Take an easy breath in through your nose, and release it out your mouth with an audible sigh. See the exhalation start to fill the balloon with your stress and worry. Repeat four more times, seeing the balloon get bigger with each exhale. After the fifth breath, release the balloon into the air. Watch it float away, carrying your stress and worry with it.

OCTOBER **3**

Write down one thing you have worried about today.

Now write down three ways you would deal
with it if your worry materialized.

1. _____

2. _____

3. _____

Feel what it's like to move from "What if?"
thinking to "If . . . then."

Let go of what others may or may not
think of you. Fix your attention on what you
know to be true about yourself.

Plan a small reward you can look forward to for
completing your least favorite task of the day.

Notice when the way you're approaching an activity is ramping up your stress level. Is there a way to go about it that is kinder to you?

Challenges await you today. On a separate piece of paper, write down a brief reminder you will need when you encounter them. For example, "Focus on what's actually happening." Carry the reminder with you for when you need it.

Observe how your body responds when you're feeling stressed. Simply see what shows up, without judging the reactions or trying to change them.

Look for an opportunity to laugh with yourself today. Appreciate the humor or absurdity that comes with your humanity.

OCTOBER **10**

Bring to mind one of your best strengths.
How can you use it today?

OCTOBER **11**

Today, let three people know that you're grateful
for them. Be as specific as you can about what
you're thankful for.

When you're wondering what difficulties life will bring you, ask yourself instead: "Am I willing to open myself to all that life has for me?"

Inhale slowly as you stretch your arms overhead. Exhale as you circle your arms down to rest in your lap. Repeat twice more and notice how you feel.

Pause today before reacting to anxiety. Are the feelings useful, or more like background noise that you can safely ignore?

Let yourself open to change. Stability is an illusion. Life is in constant flux. Release attachment to what *was* and align with what *is*.

Notice what holds you back from expressing more of yourself. Trying to please others? Fear of messing up? Unexamined habits and defenses? Take one step today toward being more fully who you are.

Close your eyes and feel the sensations in your hands. Be aware of their location in space. The actual collections of sensory experiences probably aren't hand-shaped, but are more like a cloud of sensation in the left and right hands. See how they don't map onto the picture your mind has of your hands. Breathe gently as you spend a few moments with these feelings.

OCTOBER 18

Decide how you will make the most of this
day. Regardless of what may come, this day
is yours to live.

OCTOBER 19

Assume the default position that others' actions and
emotions are due mostly to their own stuff and have
much less to do with you.

See the mind's predictions about the future for what they are—guesses that could very well prove false. Write down two mental guesses from today that miss the mark.

For a long time you've carried a worry, a regret, a resentment, or something else. What if this were the day you decided to lay it down?

OCTOBER **22**

Pick one task today and focus on the act of
completing it. Let go of thoughts about
how you're doing or what others will think.
Just do what you're doing.

OCTOBER **23**

Challenge the story that gives teeth to your
everyday fears—the one that says the only way
to happiness is to make sure everything works
out the way you want.

Life is a constant flow. Rest from
straining to control it. Simply step in.

Stand tall, feet planted firmly, head up, chest open,
shoulders relaxed, palms facing forward. Let your
mind and heart match this physical posture of
openly receiving as you go through your day.

26

Plan to take one important step in your life that anxiety has led you to avoid. Anxiety is a given whether you avoid life or enter in fully, so pick the kind of anxiety that serves you best.

27

Offer self-compassion when you're anxious. Breathe with the feelings as you gently say to yourself, "This isn't easy. You're not alone. To be human is to know anxiety. Let it be what it is."

Question the habitual assumption that you must always please other people. What evidence suggests that this belief is not really true?

When anxiety creeps up, notice any thoughts that say you shouldn't feel anxious. See what it's like to drop the "shouldn't" and simply note, "I feel anxious." Consider how unsurprising it is to have this universal human experience.

Let your breath ease you through a challenge. Inhale for a count of three and exhale for a count of five as you do the difficult thing. Breathe *with* feelings rather than trying to get rid of them.

When anxiety tells you to avoid something that's not actually dangerous, see instead if you can take even a small step toward it. Diminish fear's control over you.

NOVEMBER

Finding Peace Beyond Hope and Fear

Think about your everyday fears—about a loved one, your health, work, politics. Nearly every worry turns out one of two ways: Either it doesn't come true, and you're OK, or it does come true . . . and you're OK.

Research shows that about 90 percent of our worries never happen. Even when they do, they turn into a problem that you can manage, just like all the problems you've taken care of throughout your life.

The opposite of fear is hope: for a raise, nice weather, or that you'll find a parking space. Just as with fears, hopes have two routine outcomes: Either you get what you hoped for and your life is good (though not perfect); or you don't get what you hoped for and your life is good (and still not perfect).

It makes sense to prefer that hopes come true and that fears don't. And sometimes there are life-changing events that make life truly better or worse.

But run-of-the-mill hopes and fears tend to get a lot more weight than they deserve. Each of us has a happiness set point that is pretty consistent. External events can bump you up or down from that set point, but fairly quickly you'll return to it.

A hope fulfilled feels good for a short while and then fades into the background of life as you know it. When your hope is dashed, it doesn't leave you feeling low for long.

In a parallel way, when a fear comes true it's almost never as bad as you expected. And when a fear doesn't come true, your mind can quickly find the next thing to worry about!

As much as I want you to experience all good things in life, I also know that your well-being doesn't have to be driven by what you want or don't want. Those externals can't make or break you.

You don't have to tie your peace of mind to winning or losing. There is a peace available beyond the shifting winds of fortune.

Invest less energy in wanting everything to go your way. You can be steadfast and grounded in your well-being, like a mountain that stands strong even through the storms.

What is one task you can drop from the day's to-do list to give yourself more room to breathe?

Breathe in as you say to yourself, "Breathe in, _____," with your name in the blank. Exhale and say, "Breathe out,_____," again filling in your name. Repeat for a few more cycles.

Set a midmorning alarm for when you can take a
short break and follow these steps when it goes off:

1. Take a full breath in and then exhale for a
   count of five. Find a moment of stillness.

2. Check in with your mind. How might your
   thoughts be affecting your feelings or actions
   in this moment?

3. What is the best use of your time right now?
   Decide whether to resume what you were
   doing or pivot to something else.

In the evening, write down three challenges you overcame today. What strengths or actions allowed you to handle them? Were there other sources of support (such as a loved one) that helped you deal with them?

	Challenge	How You Handled It
1.		
2.		
3.		

If you're anxious about a task in front of you, get
started on it as soon as possible. Anxiety grows with
avoidance and shrinks when you move through it.

Keep reminding yourself when you're worried:
*I'm responsible only for what I control. Not the
future. Not my feelings. Only the outcomes
I can affect directly.*

Your day is no doubt off to an imperfect start.
You will surely have more imperfections today. Plan
in advance to go easy on yourself.

Resolve to be your own friend today. Stay by
your side, sharing your joys and offering a kind
word when you're struggling.

Go for a 15-minute walk without your phone.

Notice when you're trying not to feel an emotion. Let your resistance soften. Welcome the feeling. Watch it arrive, linger awhile, and then recede.

Let reality be the standard against which you judge your expectations, and not the reverse. Release critiques of life for somehow falling short.

Each time you catch yourself worrying about something today, write it on a list of things to worry about later. In the evening sit in a quiet place and worry about the items on your list for a full 10 minutes—seriously, set a timer. When your timer goes off, move on to other things.

NOVEMBER 13

When things are hectic all around you, find a place of stillness within yourself. At the center of every storm is an "I" that observes it all, safe and unmoved.

NOVEMBER 14

Plan three small acts of kindness for yourself that will make today a little brighter.

Breathe in for a count of four. Hold the breath in for four, and then exhale as you count to four. Pause for a four-count before you take your next breath. Repeat for a few more rounds.

Write down a task you've been putting off:

Describe a thought or mindset that
has made it harder to get started.

What is an alternative way of thinking that will help
you to complete it? For example, "I can start on it
even if I'm not sure how to do it."

Check in with yourself when you're having a tough time. Ask yourself how you're doing, and take the time to listen for how you're feeling.

Reduce the notifications on your phone so that fewer interruptions punctuate your day.

Take one minute to calm your nervous system. Breathe in gently for a count of five seconds, and then out for five seconds. Repeat for a total of six breath cycles, which equals 60 seconds. See how you feel.

What can you plan to tell yourself today that will help you to welcome anxiety rather than trying to make it go away? For example, "Anxiety is not a problem I have to solve." Write your encouraging words here.

When your mind casts itself into other times and places, reel it back in. Center your awareness on exactly where you are.

Aim to do exactly your best on an upcoming challenge. You don't need to exceed your ability. Keep in mind that you're not a machine, so your "best" will vary from day to day. Bring whatever you have in that moment.

NOVEMBER 23

No matter how many tasks you have to do today,
take them one at a time. You can handle all of it,
step by single step.

NOVEMBER 24

Bring curious awareness to the everyday experiences
that you normally don't notice, such as the sound
of closing a cabinet, the texture of a towel, or the
weight of a piece of fruit. Be fully in your world.

Plan to respond with patience when something is taking longer than you want it to. Exhale slowly as you let go of needing to get to the next thing.

Allow the good in your life to alight on your open palms, so to speak, without grasping or clinging to it. Protect your peace of mind by holding what you love lightly.

Challenge the assumption that you aren't worthy of love, or that you have to work hard to earn it. What might it be like to embrace all of yourself?

When you feel a lot of anxiety, take a minute to write down the thoughts that are feeding it. You don't need to try to convince yourself they're not true. Just recognize them as thoughts.

NOVEMBER **29**

Notice when you are taking responsibility for another person's emotions. Ask yourself if it's really your job to manage how they feel—even if their feelings are responses to something you said or did. What would it be like to let them be responsible for their own experience?

NOVEMBER **30**

Chores can feel like an obligation to be finished as fast as possible. What if instead you entered into one of these tasks as an experience worth having?

DECEMBER

Feeling Fear But Unafraid

When you feel anxiety, worry, or dread, it can seem as if the fear is all there is. We often use language like "I'm anxious" or "I'm afraid" in these situations, suggesting that the fear defines you in these moments.

And yet it's possible to feel fear and remain unmoved by it. The fear is present in your mind and body, but it doesn't capture your full experience. You're not given over to the fear.

This distinction can be hard to recognize at first. Fear and anxiety are good at capturing your awareness and dominating your attention, crowding out other experiences. They can grip your mind and make it hard to see anything else.

But there is part of you that can observe your fear responses without being changed by them. In order to know you feel fear, there must be an aspect of your awareness that is an impartial witness to the fear—and in fact, to everything you experience. That part of you is like a mirror, reflecting what you perceive without being altered by it.

This observer inside you is not afraid of your fear and doesn't need to deny it or run from it. It experiences fear as one aspect of many things that are here. Fear is present, as is the ground you stand on, the sky you see, the birds you hear. Strength and resolve are also here.

You don't have to get rid of your fear to be unafraid. You can step into the role of observer and simply notice the fear, neither trying to make it go away nor allowing it to control your actions.

When anxiety wells up inside you, acknowledge its presence without giving yourself over to it. *I see you, fear. I feel you, fear. And I choose to be unafraid.*

Count how many slow, calming breaths you take in 60 seconds. Whenever you need to unwind mentally or emotionally, pause for a *breath minute*, taking that number of relaxing, easy breaths.

Tune your awareness to notice when the mind is craving a permanent state of OK-ness. What is it longing for? True rest is found not in chasing permanence but by remembering the ephemeral nature of everything. Remind yourself that all experience is fleeting.

Spend 5–10 minutes writing about a difficult experience you recently had. Describe what happened, what you thought and felt about it, the impact it had on you, and anything else that stands out. See how you feel after this exercise.

Notice when fear is foremost as you're working
on a task, such as worrying about your child's health
while taking them to the doctor. See what it's like
to tune into love instead, like the good that your
actions can lead to.

When you're faced with a challenging task today,
release concern about what you want to gain from it
such as success, praise, or approval—things you can't
control. Focus instead on what you can give.

Sit in a quiet place and let your eyes close. As you breathe in, silently say to yourself, "I am loved." As you exhale say, "I love." Continue this process for 1–2 minutes. Orient toward the love in and around you.

Briefly describe a situation you're
worried about below.

If the outcome you fear were to happen, how would
it challenge you? What evidence suggests you would
be able to cope with these challenges?

When you're lost in the mind's fog, find yourself
through the solidity around you: a chair, the floor, a
hardcover book. Let matter ground you in what's real
and present. Repeat as often as you need to.

Embrace moments of silence throughout your day.
Rest in the space between sounds.

Practice a mantra of "We'll see" about the uncertain future. When the mind wants to worry about something, notice and welcome the unknowability.

Set a timer for 3 minutes. Before it goes off, list every challenge you remember navigating in your life so far in the space below. What does this list say about your ability to handle future difficulties?

Set your phone to Do Not Disturb for part of today to give yourself fewer prompts to look at your screen. Be curious about any thoughts or feelings that come up when you're separated from your phone.

Pause for a few moments to reconnect with your body. Sit comfortably and let your hands rest on your knees. As you breathe in, extend your right arm out to the side, stretching all the way through your fingertips. Move your eyes and head to track the position of your hand. Exhale as you watch your hand return to your lap. Repeat with your left arm, taking your time and savoring the movement. Take one more slow, easy breath as you feel what it's like to be in a body. Repeat as often as you like.

Many cultures and wisdom traditions encourage a daily practice of remembering one's mortality. Enjoy your life today as you remind yourself that eventually you will die. Let this awareness provide perspective on the day's events. What action could you take in the time you have today?

Be friendly toward your body, especially when you're struggling physically. Offer it gratitude for serving you the best it can.

When something triggers you emotionally,
stay with the feeling. Treat it as an opportunity
to discover something about yourself.

Ease off from trying to make life go your way. Let
yourself be surprised by what this day brings.

Is there something meaningful you have held
back from doing because of anxiety? Let yourself
feel the fear as you take the first step toward what
you've avoided.

Place your palms together in front of your heart.
Inhale as you slowly open your arms out wide. Exhale
as you bring them back to your heart center. Repeat
twice more. Place your hands in your lap and notice
how you feel.

Be especially aware of the smells around you. As you inhale the aromas, breathe with any memories or associations they activate.

Wear a reminder today to focus on what is in your control—a string around your wrist, a ring on your finger, or anything else that will stand out to you.

Notice when the day's problems are not as bad as they could be: the injury that prevents you from running but not walking; the fender bender that's inconvenient but not life altering; the child who is home sick but not hospitalized. Without denying the difficulty, see it in a wider context.

Shrinking from life creates anxiety about all you're missing. Diving boldly into life also leads to anxiety as you enter the unknown. Decide which anxiety is worth what it costs.

Remember that you have everything you need to face this day: your mind to think; your body to act; your heart to open and love.

There's one week left in the year. What is the most important mindset you would like to practice over the next seven days? Some examples include accepting discomfort or being willing to be imperfect. Leave a note for yourself somewhere you'll see it (such as on your breakfast table or bathroom mirror) each morning as a reminder to practice this way of thinking.

Set a timer for 4 minutes. Sit comfortably and
settle into stillness. When you feel the need to shift,
stretch, scratch an itch, or otherwise move, observe
the urge while you maintain stillness. You can apply
the same concept when different feelings arise,
observing them without necessarily
needing to react.

Embrace your imperfections today. Let them be just
another aspect of reality that you welcome.

DECEMBER **28**

Tune into the anxiety you feel. Observe it closely.
Feel its energy. Then, notice that the part of you
witnessing your anxiety is not itself anxious. The
observer within is untouched by all it witnesses.

DECEMBER **29**

Each time you step outside today, notice the change
in sound—not just the specific things you hear, but
the way the wider space affects the ambient sound
quality. Expand your awareness of what's happening
around you.

Face the day with an upright posture and your head held high. You have nothing to hide, least of all yourself.

Set a timer for 5 minutes. Close your eyes and take three easy breaths. Then open your eyes and write about this year for the remaining time. What stands out? What will you take from it? How has it challenged you and pushed you to grow?

Appendix: Common Cognitive Distortions

When you notice what your mind is up to, you'll often catch it making certain errors in the way it sees things. These errors are called *cognitive distortions*, and they're like lenses that color your experience. When you're not aware of them, they can give you a false view of reality.

Look for the following common thinking errors in your own thoughts, especially when something is causing you distress. Once you recognize what the mind is doing, you're no longer at the mercy of its distorted perspective.

COGNITIVE DISTORTION	DEFINITION	EXAMPLE
Black-or-White Thinking	Seeing things in all-or-nothing terms	"I never do anything right."
Catastrophizing	Believing the worst-case scenario must be true	"My friend is late—something terrible must have happened."
Discounting the Positive	Ignoring or minimizing evidence that goes against a negative thought	"She only wants to get together with me because she has nothing better to do."
Emotional Reasoning	Assuming that feelings are conveying important information about reality	"I feel jealous of my partner and therefore she must be cheating on me."
Entitlement	Expecting that one's actions or other factors should lead to the desired outcomes	"I should get this job because it's been my lifelong dream."
Fortune-Telling	Making predictions about what the future will bring	"I'm going to get sick from all the stress."
Mind-Reading	Assuming one knows what another person is thinking	"He thinks I'm pathetic."
Outsourcing Happiness	Giving away the ultimate power over one's well-being	"I can only be happy if my parents are proud of me."
Overgeneralizing	Thinking that what happens in one situation will apply in every situation	"I didn't get a callback so I'm never going to land any acting roles."
Personalizing	Assuming that oneself must be the cause of an outside event	"He's quieter than usual—I must have done something to upset him."
Shoulding	Believing that the desired outcome is the way things ought to be	"They should see things from my perspective."

Looking Ahead

You've reached the end of this book and the end of another year. I hope you feel good about the time and effort you've devoted to these practices, and that you've found them helpful. As we move into the New Year, it's a good time to reflect on what you want to carry forward with you.

Consider spending some time flipping through the book and reviewing the entries you found most useful. What are the practices that will really boost your well-being when you use them consistently? It might also be helpful to talk with a loved one about what you will take from this book.

Think about what you want your future self to remember when stress and anxiety start to feel overwhelming. What will help you to find peace in the middle of a storm? Allow these key practices to serve as a kind of lighthouse that can guide you when life is difficult and it's easy to lose your way.

I've offered 366 ways to practice, but the exercises boil down to three simple ideas:

1. Mind your thoughts

2. Act with intention

3. Open to the present

I often simplify these elements even further to *Think*, *Act*, and *Be*. These three little words capture well-established principles found not only in CBT but in countless wisdom traditions such as Stoicism and many forms of Eastern philosophy.

Keep these principles in mind as you look ahead to the coming year. Return to this book as often as you like, whether that means starting over with January 1, or picking it up on days when you could use a bit of guidance or encouragement. Your reset is waiting for you.

I wish you the very best that life has for you in the year ahead.

Acknowledgments

I am grateful to the many people who helped make this book possible.

To my agent and friend, Giles Anderson, for your enthusiasm for this book from the outset.

To my editor, Lauren Appleton, for your insights and encouragement. To the rest of the team at Tarcher, for your skill and efficiency.

To my friends and fellow psychologists, Joel Minden and Yael Schonbrun, for invaluable input on early drafts.

To my clinical mentor, Rob DeRubeis, for teaching me a cognitive behavioral therapy that meets people where they are.

To the readers of my newsletter, where many of these ideas and exercises were born.

To my therapy clients, for your inspiring courage and trust.

And to Marcia, Lucas, Ada, and Faye, for sharing all the days with me.

About the Author

Seth Gillihan, PhD, is a licensed psychologist who specializes in mindful cognitive behavioral therapy. His writing and therapy practice help individuals navigate common challenges like stress, anxiety, depression, sleep difficulties, burnout, and life transitions, with a focus on practical tools to support well-being. Seth served on the faculty at the University of Pennsylvania School of Medicine and now works in private practice. He is the author of several books, including *Retrain Your Brain*, *Cognitive Behavioral Therapy Made Simple*, and *Mindful Cognitive Behavioral Therapy*. He lives near Philadelphia, Pennsylvania.